Omar Sakr is the author of two acclaimed poetry collections, *These Wild Houses* (Cordite Books) and *The Lost Arabs* (UQP). *The Lost Arabs* won the 2020 Prime Minister's Literary Award for Poetry and was also shortlisted for the NSW Premier's Literary Award, the John Bray Poetry Award, the Judith Wright Calanthe Award, and the Colin Roderick Award. His first novel, *Son of Sin* (Affirm Press), was published to acclaim in 2022. Omar is a widely published essayist and editor whose work has been translated into Arabic and Spanish. Born to Lebanese and Turkish Muslim migrants in Western Sydney, he lives there still.

Non-Essential Work

Omar Sakr

UQP

First published 2023 by University of Queensland Press
PO Box 6042, St Lucia, Queensland 4067 Australia
Reprinted 2023, 2024

University of Queensland Press (UQP) acknowledges the Traditional Owners and
their custodianship of the lands on which UQP operates. We pay our respects
to their Ancestors and their descendants, who continue cultural and spiritual
connections to Country. We recognise their valuable contributions to Australian and
global society.

uqp.com.au
reception@uqp.com.au

Cover design by Josh Durham
Cover artwork by Abdul Abdullah
Author photograph by Tyler Aves
Typeset in 11.5/14 pt Adobe Garamond Pro by Post Pre-press Group, Brisbane
Printed in Australia by McPherson's Printing Group

  This project has been assisted by the
Australian Government through the
Australia Council, its arts funding and
advisory body.

A catalogue record for this book is available from the National Library of Australia.

ISBN 978 0 7022 6588 4 (pbk)
ISBN 978 0 7022 6744 4 (epdf)

University of Queensland Press uses papers that are natural, renewable and
recyclable products made from wood grown in well-managed forests and other
controlled sources. The logging and manufacturing processes conform to the
environmental regulations of the country of origin.

For Hannah, always

Contents

I

I Woke Up This Morning   3
Every Time I Visit   4
I Do Not Love Wasps   5
Salaat   6
Poem after Christchurch   8
Postscript for Poem after Christchurch   9
Dirt   10
While Observing My Jido Hold Court at the Kitchen Table   13
Iris   14
Relevant to the Day   16
What Distance Burns   18

II

On Finding the Prophet Muhammad (PBUH)
in Dante's *Inferno*   21
Dancing in Full View of the Old Masters   22
Terrorist   23
Regards   24
On Finding the Prophet Muhammad (PBUH)
in Dante's *Inferno*   25
On Finding the Prophet Muhammad (PBUH)
in Dante's *Inferno*   26
On Finding the Prophet Muhammad (PBUH)
in Dante's *Inferno*   27
Relevant to the Day   28
Relevant to the Day   29
When the Veil Parts   30
A Song of Love   31

Uncovered   33
Suppositions   35

III
When I Said Yes   39
Ritual Scroll   40
Love under Capitalism   41
Redback   43
Relevant to the Day   45
Blessed Be This Sadness   46
The Golden Hour in Unit Block 10   47
An Ode to My Future Son   48
A Muslim, Christmas   49
Inbox (1426)   51
Sundown   53
Buzzing   54

IV
Diary of a Non-Essential Worker   57
Priest of Cheesy Fries   59
Where I Am Not   60
Stay Safe   62
Relevant to the Day   63
A Reimagining   65
The Poems I Couldn't Write This Week   66
On Finding the Prophet Muhammad (PBUH)
in Dante's *Inferno*   67
On Finding the Prophet Muhammad (PBUH)
in Dante's *Inferno*   68

Your People *Your* Problem   69
No Context in a Duplex   72
Draft   73
My Enemies Need to Know   74
Shiver   75

V
The Report   79
Workshop: Borders   80
Enough   82
In the Wake of a Tragedy   83
Things that Saved My Life Lately   84
Love Poem for the Honeymoon Phase that Doesn't End   85
On Finding the Prophet Muhammad (PBUH)
in Dante's *Inferno*   87
Returning to Auburn, I Remember   88
Fruit   89
Confession   90
For a Country that Cannot Keep Its Children   91
Masks Off   92

VI
I Felt Like a Saint   95
Chorus   96
Little Fictions   97
Rooted   98
To Be Loved Like This   99
Souvenir from Another Year   100
Another Faith   101

The Right Shoe   102
Relevant to the Day   103
On Finding the Prophet Muhammad (PBUH)
in Dante's *Inferno*   104
On Finding the Prophet Muhammad (PBUH)
in Dante's *Inferno*   105
Believe   106
The Thing About Being in Love Is That   107
Child   109

Notes   111
Acknowledgements   115

I Woke Up This Morning

and asked the bird if it feels
trapped by its song, by its language
being known only as melody.
Its eloquent speech 'my home
is endless and dying' reduced to piping
notes, a shrill ringtone. I am
talking to myself. The birds are gone.
This is the problem of poetry.
We siren our warnings and the world
drowns to the sound of our beautiful
voices. I would not want it any other way.
I love a good dirge. And I am tired of being
told to claim my joy. What am I to do
with happiness? Where on earth
can happiness reside? An astonishing number
of my family are dead. An astonishing
number of my family are alive.
I woke up for this song.

Every Time I Visit

My grandmother retells the night
and the morning of her son my father
dying. He read the Quran and cried.
He left the couch for bed. Turning
in place, like her, he rarely slept.
He was alive at midnight, alive
at one, and two, and three.
For an hour she stopped checking her boy,
yoked rest. Later, she rose to look again.

He was always moving her pride her joy
from this country to his birth country—
as much man as zephyr
nothing ever pinned him down—yet now
he cupped his own cheek, he held himself still.

I Do Not Love Wasps

The wasp lies by the window as if
to beg elegy or apology for the ease
with which I smashed its wings.
I pretend not to notice & the next
day, there are two of them. I live with
the mystery, drink my ahwii, sing
slow as the glittering mound grows
& grows. One night, maddened, I
torch my burden, watch it blacken
& shrink. Later, I sweep the ash,
polish the brutal floor. As I sleep, a
new horrible arrives & is soon joined
by others. In daylight, my house is
home to the constant buzzing of
bodies living outside. I stay within.
I have enough troubles. Take this
hive, these insects I do not love,
their inescapable, mounting loss.
Baba, please stop dying. Last year
I washed your headstone, your
name, each golden number cupping
life. I claimed to understand, said I
was fine, as the jagged years passed.
I have to let go of the lies. You are
no more gone than I am here & still,
I want nothing so much as to lay
beside you, to brush your hair, smell
your silver, and to argue, again, over
what makes a man leave his son.

Salaat

The red gold prayer rug has no history. I must have bought it once, or received it as a gift. I can't be sure which action leaves a greater mark, giving or taking. The red gold prayer rug showed up in an old box full of unnecessaries. I call them unnecessaries because I left them behind, and so I condemn my grandparents or at least my own longing for what they parted from. The boy who put this box away is gone. It would be wrong to retain his memories, even if I kept his stuff. This is how I justify forgetting myself. Countries do this all the time. The red gold prayer rug glimmers, a skein of light and blood. I stretch it out flat. In the privacy of my room, I was assaulted[1] by indifference and annoyance. The red gold prayer rug doesn't care. It exists to keep skin from the earth, even if only by an inch. How many other knees graced these thick threads, mouthing Arabic? How many others pressed deep to the floor, knowing this is how close we are to God. Separated by an inch. I stand near the red gold prayer rug. I am so close to myself I can almost feel him. That bent boy, impure form, that low song, long insomnia, that refusal to dream, resentful bud, that fuckable rose, rising hour seeking salvation in a broken clock, that son shaking as the world shakes, he is as near to me as your name. The red gold prayer rug has no past, which is why I love it, though the red I could do without.

Leave me only the gold, leave a sense of value, however vague, leave me this road to the sun. I point it toward the future, which is not human, alhumdulilah, and I fold.

---

[1] I want so much to end the sentence at assaulted. At privacy. At what is taken and never restored after. I lied earlier. Taking always leaves the greater mark.

Poem after Christchurch

Postscript for Poem after Christchurch

What did you imagine there?
Write it down.
I'm sick of speaking
For monsters. Nor will I
Inhabit the victims. Speak
For yourselves, dear monsters.
Tell us what you did.

Dirt

I am tired of imaginations
I mean imagining nations
as a precursor for violence

or personal validation, soldiers
and would-be saviours, aren't you
tired, too? Settlers gotta settle, I guess

and it's true I'm part of the colony
on Dharug dirt, beneath
Dharug sky, desperate

to cling to what distances
me from my history—not heritage
but what begins with birth

at Liverpool hospital: here
is where my
Lebanese family fled

for another life. As the saying
goes: out of the frying pan
and into the slow cooker.

Tell me, who gets to own a story?
All my life I have been owned
by a story: of a prophet

named Muhammad, peace
be upon him: of the Crusades
that never ended: of Lut

peace be upon him: of a war
splitting a country like a watermelon
red seeds spat across the world:

of a baker who married a woman
in Qalamoun, and forced her to cross
the sea, fists wrapped in prayer

beads, their children, my mother
in tow: of Lebs in Liverpool, murdered
or munted, made a spectacle of,

disasters in diaspora, a colonial
headache. I'm leaving out so much
joy, of course, but also terrorism

the story noosed around our collective
neck, because this is the news &
it has to be news*worthy*, a fear

stamped into my bearded many-
storied face until *I* becomes *them*.
And I love them too, even the violent

me, even the belt that beaded
my back with blood, even the doped-
up drongo, the roided-up relo,

sis in Adidas trackies at Centrelink,
the boys at Maccas making a ruckus,
even the cops trying to fuck us

(just kidding, not them) but you
see what I mean, right? Between
our bodies, mythic stories lie

like sleeping lions & few know
how to cross without waking the pride
that eats the vulnerable alive.

Once I believed I could make myself
free, at least for a time, here, in language;
that was before I knew of people

with barbed-wire hands
hungry to reach out & touch anyone
regardless of the cost,

who rend desperate mouths
& whisper over the muffled shouts
I'm doing this for you.

While Observing My Jido Hold Court
at the Kitchen Table

You think I am sad
because of the slaughter.
Because of my mother
and absent father.
Because of all the love
that never was, or left us.
It is so precious, the idea
sadness needs a trigger.
Like every time I'm called
a sand n— ruptures
the happy. It's not true.
This is the signature
condition of the Arab.
Even at Heaven's door
we say, *Is that all?*

Iris

If any room can be said to be mine,
surely it is this one, the desk at which I perform
my agonies, and yet my wife

though she uses it less, still can reveal
compartments I never knew existed as if
her presence alone expands the world.

I thought I was present. I thought I knew
how to occupy a space. To understand it
intimately, if not possessively.

I fear to have not known every part
is not to have known it at all—we
could all be strangers all the time.

My god, the joy of that. The terror.
We're not ready
to love each other that much.

The sun is streaming through the window.
An awful line except now
your gaze is diverted and I can try again.

Sometimes choosing not to see is a survival
tactic. Sometimes I am in love
with oblivion—leaving myself behind—

through the startlement of creation
in the black eyes of the rat scooting
across the neighbour's fence outside,

or the blank circles of unrendered faces
above the sidewalk making everyone
both guest & ghost. I refuse

to put glasses on this life, all of it
is a brilliant distraction from the wound
O to be the light coming out

to know the room, to make clear what is
beyond it, to invent a wife kind enough
to reveal what I missed.

Relevant to the Day

I read Dorothy Porter last night and her
surrender to desire slunk into my sleep
left teeth marks on my dreams. My unit is full
of desiccated

flowers a breath could undress. Outside: the light,
pink and blue, an elevated spring sea that
apes a seasonal surety no longer
available. I

keep the doors shut, and still the wounded world spreads
over the breakfast table, daring us, again,
to eat it, the futility of witness.
They called the slaughter

an accident, as if drones can kill by chance.
Call it what it is: families destroying
other families. I don't know how to mourn
an accident *and*

a family. You choose one or the other.
I'm sick with overwhelming intimacies.
I don't understand how we are functioning.
We've shared everything

humans can share. Sometimes, like today I ask
even love to leave while I'm naked and I
put a door between us, the smallest distance
I can bear and you

say one flower is still alive, seeking sun
it bends toward its outer kin, kept apart
by foggy panes of glass and as you say it
trembling, inching close,

I know it, the peril of belief, that something
unlikely only moments ago could so
swiftly burst into being, and this is why
I insist on love.

What Distance Burns

Smoke softens the trees, a swift omen scented before seen.
It warps what it brings, from the sun to grief.

I stir on the stoop I rent. All around me wasps shimmy,
Orange alphabet of knives. I call them *father* and *son*

Until my tongue blisters. I chew the queen into bits
And for a moment, we understand each other

Her children and I, the way a believer understands God:
As a largeness capable of being

Stung. Out of stillness I come to marvel
At my survival, the stupendous absurdity of breath.

I tremble so violent I lift off the ground, a man
Dripping between earth and sky with only a mother

Left in life—what luck—and men I will never call
Baba. Soon I am high enough to see the limits of burning

The pall dispersing over waves, the end arriving
As always, on the edge of an unfathomable wing—

In the long vanishing blue I smile a migrant smile
Knowing we look our best as we leave.

On Finding the Prophet Muhammad (PBUH) in Dante's *Inferno*

I lift him out, whole and perfect.
Said told me he would be here, chained by Dante
To the eighth circle of hell, bettered only by the devil himself.
The Paris Review recapped this canto in 2014, saying
Read along! This week: Mohammed torn asunder.
And so he was, again, 'cleft from chin to colon'. In summary
We are assured this is a marvellous mangling.
I cannot abide (t)his pain. I have taken him out,
Wounding the text, the ancient imagining,
And write myself into it so asunder I tear,
Guts and shit spilling down my legs. Omar,
Foolish provocateur, no prophet, but sower
Of schism and scandal, yes, he belongs here. Now
Do not use his name if you do not love him: use mine.

Dancing in Full View of the Old Masters

Whenever we are watched, I become
a painting, that is to say, ornate
or something framed, a being edged
and if not quite hung
on a silver hook then at least heavy
enough to impress upon any surface

especially another body.
What does it mean to be seen
as art when something buyable
is something burnable
and something relevant
is ignorable? I tell you not to
make me, but with every kiss
on my hairy nipples

another line emerges
another colour is invented
one only we know
and you say don't worry this is not
for a fucking museum and even if it was
don't we owe it to the world
to keep going when everything else
stops to behold us

Terrorist

Do not come to me for transformation
I am no funhouse mirror, nor a lake;
I am not the riven skin of the earth
nor the fey chameleon sky. All I have
are questions without answer. What
if Icarus was a refugee fleeing his father,
what if he flew not from ambition but fear,
a suicide dive upward—what if he welcomed

the fire? What if he had a bomb
strapped to his chest, and wanted to rain
pieces of sky down on the othering dirt?
This is why I grow no wings. I am terrified
everyone will see I am a flightless angel
falling up, as far from any father as I can get.

Regards

Dear father dear fascist dear fetter dear farmer
dear denial dear defiler dear despot dear artist
dear all determined to imagine my relevant
body: it's not that I want to be seen or heard,
understood or known, it's that I want the killing
to stop. OK, I want it all, so what? I am a mote
of dust and still some say I'm seen too much,
heard too much, I am all the way in the way
trying to fit my mouth over death. Go ahead and
loose the blast, unfreeze the march! Make me
a martyr, baby. Every poet is a failed
revolutionary & it's so embarrassing. The truth
is, I don't want to waste another day with work.
Let's make that word irrelevant. You choose
which: work, waste, want, revolution, hate, I.
I'm begging you to make me irrelevant. Did
you never stop to consider what re levanting my
body would do? Did you never worry that
I might love my clothes or that, once given,
we could never be naked again? You'll have to
speak up, I'm wearing a towel.

On Finding the Prophet Muhammad (PBUH) in Dante's *Inferno*

A big beautiful Quran
joins my home, song
book of the untranslatable:
faith. It keeps raining.
I trace the calligraphy it makes.
I have at least one prayer
entirely memorised
but cannot tell you where
it leads. Any of the paths
left by the water on the window
could take you to the same place.
My ignorance makes this Surah large
as the world, larger even—my god no
wonder they call this a dark worship.

A unique guilt
joins my home, song
of the urban slant:
kin in pain eat
carceral lights.
I heaven
teen memories,
watch lonely
lads. Any path
left by the war
could take us.
My ignorance makes
the world large—my god
calls this a dark worship.

On Finding the Prophet Muhammad (PBUH)
in Dante's *Inferno*

I slip into my insolence, sleek as an eel.
I have walked so many ways around God I can tell you
Holiness is a roundabout
With a thousand exit points labelled doubt;
Like the boy who unzipped my pants
In my sleep, who broke the zipper of my sleep
So I have lost the measure of rest since;
Like my father leaving before I knew him or could speak;
My body forever unkneeling to pray
Unless there's a zipper in front of me, a boy in front
Of me a ghost a beckoning a gate where, perhaps,
If I open wide enough I will be able to wake,
Again, and still, soaked as I am in shame—still
I care about my Prophet's name.

On Finding the Prophet Muhammad (PBUH) in Dante's *Inferno*

A lover undresses, with permission.
Picture the body becoming real.

> I picture becoming real intimate.
It is strange to think of legs as closed.

> I open my legs for strangers. I widen,
stretch. What belongs here? Don't say a door.

Instead of belonging, I eat the door,
> make an animal flap for the four-legged.

I'm on all fours. Ass slapped. An animal flap.
> Violence begets. Love circumvents. I swallow

> my would-be begottens. Love, this violence.
To all doormen I say ahlan wa sahlan.

Man, this door shudders. Familiarly, easy.
I undress permission with splintered hands.

Relevant to the Day

My sister gave birth to a jaundiced boy
and weighed his yellowing with my name as
though four letters could bridge years of silence.
Like me, he was an unexpected son.
Ever since then, a trio of moons at least,
my lover and I have argued about
the last loud gasps of this palliative world—
should we bring life into what is ending?
No one is working. The heat has a long
monologue, like the cold; the landlord
stays immune to our suffering, and we
are still the best off of all our people
unto the beginning of our species.
Today we fucked desperately, queries

unresolved, a drama worth our wildest
efforts. I want the neighbours to hear us.
Their son does constant laps of the units,
his basketball a lopsided drumbeat,
lonely and irregular as my hips.
Through him I know that by virtue of not
killing kids, one can feel like a parent,
and reluctantly I become my mum,
casting evidence of breath as kindness.
I know, too, through the daughter I refused,
that to thwart a child feels like parenthood,
a long assertion of control and yet
I swear this is not an elegy, not
now she never leaves me, my girl to be.

Relevant to the Day

I place my father's grave
into the GPS, I am eighteen
minutes away
from him. My love
gathers eucalyptus leaves
to lay over his new skin.
Halfway there I revert
to memory and take us
to the wrong plot: here
I am always losing
my bearings. The flowers
and weeds know how
to say grief in every language
made as they are to root &
rot. I drift through the bobbing
falling syllables,
to the absence I have
always known—Baba,
I whisper the Fatiha, kneel
in the weeds, and pray
for a direction that includes us both.

When the Veil Parts

We hooked up six weeks after the funeral. That must be how long it took my departed father to beg God for his son to fall in love with a woman. I never imagined a life like this, one in which I am happy, and knowing it has ruined the future. We can only dwindle now. I try not to bother you with this foreshadowing. I watch movies. I earn small dollars. Count down the hours. Lap the block of decaying animals. Avoid the bees beginning their dizzy deliverance around helpless flowers. I do not call my mother. I laugh eerily at whatever my brother sends me, in fact, as soon as I see his name, humour wedgies my spine. I fuck you on good days and bad. We argue about the dishes. I use dildos to teach myself new raptures when I am alone. This has nothing to do with your womanhood, it is mine, a long handheld heaven because I haven't met a man I trust enough to deliver me there, and this is one way we are both women. You ask me what this is about as I write it. Mandarins? I lie and taste citrus. I don't know how to be anything other than queer and sad. I need to map a way out of this unexpected complication and all I can think to say is ta'aburnee. We part sometimes, and you work and sleep as I do, but these are false previews of absence, predicated on return. I no longer look at mandarins except as an omen for loss. It's not all bad news. My father, God bless him, already proved that when life ends love enters.

A Song of Love

for Gabriel Fernandez

My heart is acting up. It's the altitude, they said
making my guts dance and whirl. I am oceans
away from you thinking, we could have had a son
a girl an androgynous beauty. I know I can hold
chubby fingers as well as any parent. The Pacific, love,
hides a universe: billions of species in the dim

the dark blue-green. In the deep, the dimming
world shines with eyes, hooks, wrecks and acid.
The universe, our polluted waters, hides love.
The biggest heart to ever beat stays in the ocean.
I've been reading too much. Trying to cover an old
absence. The day we erased the possibility of a son

you left my side a dozen times, shaking, the sun
a pale, violent wave. It's okay I whispered to him
to her, it's okay. *We did the right thing.* I am cold
with certainty. Habibti, I'm weeping from what I read
about a boy, on the other side of the ocean,
all of eight years of age, and unknown years of love,

whose parents tortured him for days & days. Beloved,
what heaven can justify the abuse of a son?
They beat and burned him. Fed him an ocean
of shit and his own vomit in a room made dim
by what was done to him. He was eight, I said.
Small, gentle. There is only so much I can hold

of any loss, I think. Or: loss is all that I can hold.
I could have curled my body around him, love.
I could have shown him the sea, its long lucid
dreams, how we have filled it with the poison
that lives in us, and how despite that, we swim
in it still, the spectacular, heart-filled ocean.

I'm not fooling anyone, I know. O cyan
O blues, when will you consider us told,
the last feeling felt? Don't say when the stars dim,
or that sorrow's continued play relies on love.
I have no right to grieve this, he was not my son,
as the world is not my world and what is said

is debatable, because everything ownable is reducible, even love,
my ocean, this tide brimming with gargantuan music, our reason
for being, can you hear it, bub? Listen again to what I've said.

Uncovered

The train shivers my body over the tracks.
Whole swathes of country become unseen.

The land and I will share a sigh of relief
when, at last, one of us blinks.

To be perceived is such ugly work.
I try to relax into midnight's trench.

The leather seat beside mine holds a woman
for a time and then empties.

I was warned about this, not to touch
the absence. It will be filled by another

kind of warmth if left alone; the train
occasionally whispers such things.

I write my father's name on the window,
touching the absence. It is human

to spoil potential. I remove him and return
to witness: the night making love to dirt,

to river, to copse and corpse. The moon
eats the song of release, white arches.

I cover the longest leagues in darkness
with strangers all marked for different

departures. I miss them, the unwashed
and overly perfumed, and then, I don't.

The city nears, bright with death.
I can smell its breath from here.

I look away. There are too many eyes,
a surplus of stars, real and false, all abuzz

claiming that I, yes you, can be the centre
of a universe. I was once, and now I'm not.

Suppositions

I suppose I am a student of the world and all
its subtle variations. I suppose I want an ode
to the mundane, yet glory keeps veiling
my mother's ashtray, a cracked slab
she either stole from a temple or was gifted
by a man bamboozled in a boutique store.
I suppose glory flickers. Glory ghosts.
Sometimes I lick around the coffee cup
lapping up the omens and summon
onto my tongue the sorrow that made
everything possible. I suppose
I sound religious. I suppose I am doomed
to finding angels on my shoulders anyway.
Nobody needs my hands raised as supposed
shield yet I keep raising them. I suppose
this existence, this country, this coast
where beached angels gleam enormous
blowholes sputtering a final fitful prayer.
I would have spared them once, but no longer,
bodied as I am with everyone I forgot to look after.
My mistake was in supposing to study the world,
instead of love it. I walked away from the landed
celestials, who even dying were so full they
burst to feed generations of bird, fish, crab.
This is the measure of holiness I suppose,
how much we can give at our last.

When I Said Yes

I am a child.
He is muscled, adult
intent, ready to bruise.
The sun, too, adults the sky.
I see it through the blinds,
the blue bend, low white.
Back to his waiting eyes.
His long want. 'Let me.'
I cup my no. I hold it
close. He shifts nearer.
'Come on.' Again. 'Let me.'
The blankets spell my no.
The walls are papered with my no.
My mouth is closed.
I have never seen need like this
a thickness that begs.
Come on. Let me. Come on. Let me
come. I had given him a morning
of my no and then, Lord, I had my first
reason to ask for your forgiveness.

Ritual Scroll

I'm drunk on damage: floods, wildfires,
a local death. Beside me, my lover stirs and
the timeline leaps—to a cockatoo perched on
a colleague's balcony, its parted beak, fluffed
head cocked, eye dark, crest bright—then back
to an unarmed protestor killed by an oppressor,
whereupon I darken. Turn away. Rub my arm,
almost fancying talon marks line the skin as if
I, and not a rail, had held the feathered whole,
the raucous heart and long wings. I am
not yet awake. An inferno tickles the bottom
of my tongue. I sneeze and a town drowns.
Another body is on top of mine. I don't want to
see him, not his curly hair, not the scar, or chip
in one of his teeth. Don't tell me the angle
of the bullet that dove into his eye. My lover
coaxes us into the shower, shifting me,
the dead, our bird-friend into the bathroom, into
the falling water. The bird takes to
the curtain pole. I wash myself. I wash him
slower. His head tilts back, filling with rain
that pours out his mouth, nose, and ears. I clean
his dick, his pits, his ass, until the steam erases
us. I arrive here in the wake. I wonder who
has carried me into the shower with them
this morning, if these texts mean anything,
if they too were so foolish as to forget to love
their lover, to even say good morning, to look and
see they are gone.

Love under Capitalism

The new joint around the corner keeps changing
its name. I get it.
I am afraid of growing old.

I can't afford this face for long, this place for long.
I still invite people in.
The barista wants to know me. I want to trust

his intentions, his *sup* as I sip what he made
and feel a little more alive.
I shiver at *the usual* delivered by his dimples.

Large cap? Desire hissing. *Four forty-five.*
It feels wrong to say
Don't ask me to be human. This is a transaction

only. I need to preside over when I am more
than money moving
between machines. This is not my first

coffee of the day and won't be my last. I slide
my hand over
the silver band of my fade and imagine it as his

a distance closed, as a tug at my trackies.
He needs to be
talking. To be more than a service. A silence.

The cost of this moment is greater
than either of us
knows or cares to think about for the other.

The radio squawks: there's been another attack.
A crack tears through the café.
I take what I ordered and leave with what I need:

no expectation of a return.

Redback
after Nikki Giovanni

The strangers living in my house know death
has taken up residence under our doorstep.

They were anxious to keep this secret,
aware of how much I value my life &

how willing I am to kill to preserve it.
Death is small and unconcerned

with you, they said. Simply step
over him into life. Your day awaits.

I can't stop thinking about my mortal
enemy. How dare he live so close

and take comfort from my home,
what a villain. Every day now

I let the doorway hold me
and linger over the crack he slumbers in.

Death will only come out at night
they tell me, these concerned strangers,

he keeps to himself otherwise.
Such wondrous naiveté.

If left alone death will have children
and his children will be hungry.

Life demands it. Who could be
so generous as to deliver their body

into the mouth of the wolf? To say, let him
slobber on my skin. Don't drive him away.

I am not a generous man. I will crush death
if I can. Sometimes I fear

I might be his child, true product
of his teaching. What if I look and see only myself?

Is that what the strangers saw when they spoke
quietly with death out on the moonlit stoop?

I envy those small moments when they give
themselves over to the dark, their soft laughs.

I want their goodness, I want
for this kindness to not be strange.

I tell all this to the moon who dies so often
and must know something of the affair

and the moon in pity tears a strip
off her black blanket and gifts to me

a blindfold, so I can re-enter my home
unafraid to call those I live with by their names.

Relevant to the Day

The story of a murder crosses the globe
in a heartbeat or breath
and people everywhere are talking.
The act of dying opens so many chests.
Outside, Poe stares at me from within a raven
so I shout, 'Remove yourself, stupid man!'
Due to what I have read, every black bird
is weighed down by a sickly sad man.
How depressing. I shake the image into a caw,
tree tops, an unsolvable mystery.
Anyway, people are grieving a music lost,
and I listen as they fall deeper into themselves.
The Venn diagram of those who believe
love at first sight is a myth & people who weep
the instant they learn of a loved one passing
is a perfect circle—how knowledge enters
the body and when it leaves are the concerns
of those most determined to make
their own meaning. By coincidence,
it is they who wind up faithless, alone
with their hands and chance. The Arctic is melting,
a phrase I do not understand. Can anyone?
To stand under means 'to be close to'
and we cannot be close to what vanishes,
which is the world, or at least the parts I live on
and that I must admit I enjoy. Here, to vanish is
to become unfamiliar, hostile, strange—a polar bear
in Aldi, a headless galloping, a name unending.

Blessed Be This Sadness

after Les Murray

Weeping open on the train one day
I learn no one speaks to the sorrowful
except to say *I'm sorry* or *I've been there*
or to caw like some useless bird. No one
has been to this place, my sweet dark sea.
You may have your own, a waterless rock
or else some other reflection of world,
a bedroom, a garden of knowledge, a mouth.
Mine is not a dog, not apart, think anxious
sea full of unique fish, crustaceans
and algae that wash up on a glass beach.
I visit the shore every morning afraid
it will disappear without my care, my
soft light. When I'm there, I hold
the necklace of wounds my mother gifted
me, tiny tragedies, accidental histories,
each one a jewel, amethyst of fist, topaz
abortion, and oh the blood diamonds
of neglect. Every wound here is a window
back to life, little lungs pumping air
into this beautiful void. And it is beauty.
Many moons of pale pink and blue hang
in the sky, each one a halo. I love
this grief-wrought hole. All that I have
lost lives in it. Together as never
in life, we swim, we school, we
sink in moon and diamanté sand. Bone
dry, I leave wet footprints wherever I go.
Back in the carriage, the necklace is heavy
as a solar system and absolutely ordinary.

The Golden Hour in Unit Block 10

My friends tell me the day's most spectacular band of light
occurs at its end, before the bend, the long delve into dusk,
and that it hits my bathroom in a burst of glory that is
perfect for selfies. I believe them, though I never knew
beauty to keep a schedule. I try to fix it in mind, to be
ready for its arrival, and I miss it every time, finding the
sun's leavings or the dimpled blues of night instead. I try
to capture the self, like everyone else, regularly, and when
I do, I position the camera just so, the body just so, aiming
not for vanity but familiarity, what I recognise as my golden
hour. I practise my death like this. After doing the laundry,
putting all the empty versions of myself out to dry, I take
photos of my naked ass, my huge haunches & fancy I know
how to reveal what is hidden. What we hid used to be called
intimate: a low cry, an uncle's creeping, how little we had
to eat. Now every intimacy fights for space on the line.
The Hills hoist can carry only so much of our undressing.
I resist placing my wife's soft parts here in the sun among
nameless men, midnight mementos. I need every morsel
of tenderness I've earned yet still you ask for more. The you
is poetry. The you is I. I've fathered several children who
do not know me. This nightmare recurs. When the dark is
absolute, my love crosses from her side of the bed to mine,
burrowing under my body with cold hands and colder feet,
drawn across dream to my warm slowing, my gathered
hours. She cannot sleep without the pressure, she says. I
cannot sleep at all. Alone with my other half, I am a restless
moon begging for a man's heel, a band of light made purely
to praise another.

An Ode to My Future Son

The bed is mussed, the sheets distressed
snakes. My wife hisses within her nest,
stop kicking the blankets off! As if I
control the dream. I control the dream
as much as you control your mother
from her womb: not at all, and also
completely. When you move within her,
she gasps in delight, calling me over to feel
what she feels, this future. I am too slow
or late or else you still as I near, like any deer
faced with a father. He always kicks as you go,
I hear. And now I know what the dream is,
why I—the son of a zephyr—will never still.
Even in sleep, I bound toward what recedes.

A Muslim, Christmas

The streets are empty-ish.
Ish is for my body
the believer, the lonely.
I head toward departure.
Long one-eyed spectres
hunch over the earth
and each tree has around it
a darker deeper life.
Few shops are open: solitary
yellows adorn a doorway or two
amid dormant heavens
(I call any abundance heaven now) saying
welcome in Mandarin and, later, Arabic.
I move past the beckoning oasis.
I am not looking for a home
all prior attempts failed—
I aim to find the heaven of me,
the we who linger at stations
to hear a loop of human voices
skip over silence or sink into it,
to relish the ripple that makes absence
visible. We move through enormity
and feel our crowdless edges
with the hand of an ancestor, perhaps
brushing the backs of our necks so
we tilt up to see a migrantory heaven
pummel the sky and disappear.
Elsewhere, beloveds
gather, ready to unwrap

a gift beneath
the semblance of a tree
or the memory of pine, still green,
and though I have one
a family I mean a queerness
I cannot abide leaving
the city without a body
to trouble its making.
I have no destination
in mind—how sacred it is,
this not knowing, how divine
to walk in this world as an ish.

Inbox (1426)

1426 is my new zero, the cannibal counting point.
I cannot see what came before, I cannot remember
when there weren't lifetimes waiting
to be read. Eventually, everything you miss
becomes part of your beginning. Start here,
with the next missive: 1427, a promo
for a movie about the first witch hunt
in Switzerland. The logline: *Every witch serves
the devil, and every devil is a man.*
It's the kind you watch hoping no one survives.
Increasingly, these are the only stories I see.
1427: a petition to boycott the movie.
1427: a petition to boycott the boycott.
1427 keeps me from getting back to zero. I love
my new one—distinguished, particular, alone,
its constant renewal. Whenever I return
to 1426 I feel relief, and anguish.
My losses are like this. Reconstituting the ground.
Zero is my father, a shrouded man, then my uncle,
grandparents, cousins, friends and others.
I don't know when this happened, when Baba
became a fact not a feeling. Sometimes he lurches
out of zero and kisses me rough, his cologne
a spicy mist, and there is no reality except
his nicotine-stained hands. 1427, breaking news:
a boy I resemble cuts his rope and what happens
next is up for conjecture. As I fall
my small fugitive numbers flinch
from name to numeral, figurative to figure,

& I long for a new unbearable loss to hold,
or if not a loss, love, and if not a love, hate—
the things we braid and bind for the drop.

Sundown

Interrupt the muse: leave the room.
I am going through something here I text
and she says, I am what goes through you.
Each day I part a sheer black veil to leave
my house. Watch it shiver together to seal
the hole afterward. It has to do with magnets
or atoms, or love. I made that up. Love,
not the veil I placed so deliberately over
my door to temper delicate dangers—
anything that can enter or touch my skin.
Weeks can pass without the black membrane
moving, actually, and if it is pierced at all
it is only by memory. I let the record play.
The sky is saying goodbye again,
its favourite word, all promise, all
translation, and you know how that goes,
the forever echo. I have a dozen lives
at my fingertips, like any spider, and none
of them are enough. I crawl around the empty
lip of a slender Coke bottle left by the window.
I build a tiny glass web. I will catch the sky
in it, some particulate blue, at least, before dark.
Oh daily diminishment, oh father, take my light.

Buzzing
a poem written in The Arabic, after Marwa Helal

mouth as double to wings with
night the wasp would I
lights fake all & darkness agitate
my razor my syntax
madness sweet

swelling
—hours mythic against
—lurk moons & Arabs & spells wherever
power oppressive its puncture I
tongue my movement

aloft serenade a
ض of language the in dancing
far as dad to close as not
fact in mother as away
I would nowhere &

leave or body a sting
might you except mark a
blessed the note
wake my in stillness
murmurs fearful hushing

IV

Diary of a Non-Essential Worker

Did you know violins can shake the earth? Such sweet vessels, tiny planetary throats. I was sent an orchestra. They made music a sorrow, a soaring that shivered the dirt. I followed the notes to a barbarism. The composer said he created the beautiful hour as a space to think about war, and I heard my mother's name, a dark cascade of her, I saw again the clamour behind her manner, her harrowed glamour; I am claiming all of it now not as a violence, but as an inevitability, always justifiable. I guess I don't want to lose her, no matter the bruises. I haven't seen her in weeks, a memory of cherries, a perishable delight. I stay home, she stays home, and with this distance we become old battlefields, able to appreciate our damages without adding to them. How lucky we are to have homes. How likely it is we will lose them. Months ago we couldn't breathe and smoky miracles pulverised the sky, our fussy lungs. Everything is a miracle when you are alive. I am learning that against my will. Today I was sent a pink dwarf kingfisher, a bird thought extinct for over a century, and still, it was someone's job to look for her, someone waited, camera in hand, for a glimpse of a glorious beak. Outside, I hear the camaraderie of ordinary wings, the chatter of birds we call pests. They don't seem to mind the lockdown. I dare say they are having fun, a lark. I call my landlord, ask for a reprieve, and hear only birdsong. He's having fun. I walk out into the park, where, months prior, a man was stabbed near to death; I sit on the bench close to the stain his blood left and receive a text reminding me to care about Kashmir, and Gaza, and our Uyghur brothers and sisters, who I never stopped caring about, and for whom my care did nothing. Forgive me, I sometimes mistake grief for care. The orchestra follows me under the foliage, the violins unrelenting, the world shaken to their curvature, their high-strung demands, as I sift through the scattered lyric of my shattered life to find a way to love a woman, and the birds weave and whirl in the green, laughing at this non-essential work.

Priest of Cheesy Fries

Under familiar lights I shove the cheap
burger in my mouth. Fingers diamond with salt, time
drips down the side. Last night on a menu
I saw lobster, flirted with fancy, decided I couldn't eat
a dish so rich with this body. I'm haunted
by all that I never had, never satisfied
with what I do: a genesis in grease.

Nobody stays in these eateries. I keep returning
to flood my arteries. The food is forgettable.
Loneliness feels like family once
you have known it long enough, once you've fought it,
hated, and come to love it. Nobody wants to be
seen here. Dear temple of invisibility
fortress of saturated fats, thank you
for killing me so slowly no one calls it harm.

Where I Am Not

I ask the new migrant if he regrets leaving Russia.
We have dispensed already with my ancestry.
He says no. For a time, he was depressed. He found
with every return he missed what he left behind.
A constant state of this. Better to love by far
where you are. He taps the steering wheel of his car,
the hum of the engine an imperceptible tremble
in us. When he isn't driving, he works tending
to new trees. I've seen these saplings popping
up all over the suburbs, tickling the bellies
of bridges, the new rooted darlings of the State.
The council spent a quarter mil on them &
someone, he—Lilian—must ensure the dirt
holds. Gentrification is climate-friendly now.
I laugh and he laughs, and we eat the distance
between histories. He checks on his buds daily.
Are they okay? They are okay. They do not need
him, but he speaks, and they listen or at least
shake a leaf. What a world where you can live off
land by loving it. If only we cared for each other
this way. The council cares for their investment—
the late greenery, that is, not Lilian, who shares
his ride on the side. I wonder what it would cost
to have men be tender to me regularly, to be
folded into his burly, to be left on the side
of the road as he drove away, exhausted. Even
my dreams of tenderness involve being used
& I'm not sure who to blame: colonialism,
capitalism, patriarchy, queerness or poetry?

Sorry, this is a commercial for the Kia Sportage
now. This is a commercial for Lilian's thighs.
He is taking me all the way back, around
the future flowering, back to where I am not,
to the homes I keep investing in as harms.
I should fill them with trees. Let the boughs
cover the remembered boy, cowering under
a mother, let life replace memory. Lilian,
I left you that day, and in the leaving, a love
followed. Isn't that a wonder and a wound?
Tell me which it is, I confess I mistake the two.
I walk up the stairs to my old brick apartment
where the peach tree reaches for the railing,
a few blushing fruits poking through the bars
eager to brush my leg, to say linger, halt.
I want to stop, to hold it for real, just once
but I must wait until I am safe.

Stay Safe

Helicopters cough in circles above the city.
The city circles our beds. My neighbour's
coughs mark the hours. I'm not going
anywhere. I've been everywhere. I circle
the block again. I yell *stay safe* through
the walls. The demand is a buried plea.
The world is in my pocket and I can't stop
touching it. I'm told to beware the danger
in touch and air as if I haven't died under
a sweet hand a hundredfold or returned
to life on another's fetid breath. I do as
I'm told. I pass the coughing cops and the
coughing church and the coughing magpies
and the coughing tanks and the coughing
beggar and I don't touch anyone, I swear—
still, the silence spreads, it infects my sleep,
my fenced faith my shadow my home my
tomb. I record this loving aloneness. Wind
it back. Hover there, beating at the air hard
enough to keep memory at bay.

Relevant to the Day

After a traffic altercation in Western Sydney

I don't have anything hopeful to say, love. In Bankstown
my cousin was shot in the head. My wife thinks she can
have road rage anywhere. Wants to know why I couldn't
speak. I show her my mouth full of bullets and she insists
some people deserve to be yelled at, get the finger.
I swallow the lead. I'm not brave enough to imagine
the future anymore. I lost it when I was fifteen and another
cousin was stabbed to death on the street.

I lay in bed, thinking of graves and sleep without entering
either, alone in the awful splendour of night's arms, trying
to picture what comes next. Without success, I can only
dare to see as far as tomorrow: the laundry if the sun is out
long enough and the line is free. Charcoal chicken, toum,
sex. A wet welt. Still, always in silence, my favourite
countryside. This is progress. Millions suffer and die in the
course of my progress.

I grew up believing this was normal, expected. I want to
draw a line from one suffering to another but people keep
getting in the way. I saw a parade of empty fridges in
Lebanon yesterday. Prayed one of the sad aunties standing
next to the emptiness was not mine. I know distance better
than I know her face, and so, they all became her. I sent
money through my kinship network and who knows whose
mouth it fed? Kholto, I'm sorry, I know money is not bread.

They say a famine is coming, no, spreading. There is always a famine somewhere. I have one deep in my heart I am familiar with ignoring. The motherland is begging her children to return. The borders are closed, fridges empty, shelves bare, and I keep thinking at least one of my mothers wants me now, or I'm so full I could vomit, so full I can't move or, when I can, I will go and curl up inside one of those fridges, I will whisper, eat as much as you can stomach, sweet siblings and I will thank God, for once, that I must put my body where my poetry is.

A Reimagining

I do have a hopeful love. In Bankstown, my cousin saw ahead the road to anywhere. I show my wife my mouth full of let's and she insists some people deserve to swallow, be led. I'm brave enough to imagine the future. More. When I am fifty, I eat another sin on the street.

I lie in bed, thinking of raves, and see, without entering, the full splendour of night, arms, trying to come. Success. Now I can dare as far as the sun is long and free. Charcoal chicken, toum, sex. Awe. Till, aywa, license, my favourite countryside. This is progress. Millions use my progress.

I grew up normal, expected. I draw a line from one offering to another; in getting, people keep the way. I saw a parade of figs in Lebanon. Prayed the aunties next to it were mine, my kin, all fed. Kholto, my dear fam, I'm reading there is always a me somewhere I am familiar with.

The motherland is her children. Return the borders, empty selves bare, and keep my mothers full, so full I can move when I will, I can curl up inside his ridge, whisper, take as much as you can stomach, sweet bliss, and I will thank God, for once, that I put my body where poetry is.

The Poems I Couldn't Write This Week

The poem about two Afghan boys whose throats were opened by Australian men. The cynical poem about there being no reason. The poem where they still live. The eco poem about the river the cut boys were left in. The enraged poem about the graceless water. The war poem on the devastation of Empire. The war poem about artists whose taxes paid for the devastation. The family poem about my mother once again not meeting me at the cemetery. The redacted poem using military language like it can be salvaged. The spiritual poem exploding over intended and unintended targets with no effect. The transactional poem that requires an effect. The bilingual poem that swallows God. The servile that licks the boot of the buyer. The political that invents a moral arc of democracy. The ancestral that won't let the dead rest. The dark that refuses to kill the poet. The domestic that imagines itself as separate from all the others. The poem that poems. Inna lillahi wa inna ilayhi raji'un. The mistranslated: verily we belong, and verily we return.

On Finding the Prophet Muhammad (PBUH) in Dante's *Inferno*

I am relieved
by the revelation
that some people
lack a mind's eye
to see what we
imagine words
say. 2% of humans
keep text as text
& this is beautiful
except of course
for all the photos
and art determined
to see for us & ensure
nobody misses out.

I relive
the reveal
that poems
nakedly
sew a West
in words.
A % of humans
see this
as beautiful.
Coexecutors
of the fall
narrate to
foster neuroses
& issue dooms.

On Finding the Prophet Muhammad (PBUH) in Dante's *Inferno*

I am reminded why his name is followed always
By *peace be upon him.* Not only can he be troubled
Like anyone else, even to him the implication remains
That peace is not guaranteed nor over a body lain,
Though perhaps it is a state that can be invoked
Or persuaded into allowing an alien—that is, human—
Into itself. Chomsky says persuasion is a soft violence,
That we should all of us go as we wish to go, at pace
Or not, as desired, and this is how I know Hell is my place
For am I not even now drumming this silken fist
Into your tenderness? Am I not a priest of telling
You that you are There and I am Here, my breath
Warm against your cheek? Truly language is my master,
Snapping at my heels as I leap into the bush, a-lather.

Your People *Your* Problem

Fellow flotsam, what makes a person
a person? The animals are asking.

Friends, what makes a citizen a
citizen? The people are barking.

Fiends, what makes a nation a nation?
The massacred know the murderers

pretend not to.
I consider this from within my inbox.

Schrödinger's poet, dead and alive,
a stupid rhetorical device:

the box is brimming full of ghosts
and the splendour of seedless soil.

Isn't potential grand? Like a mother
who is yet to *be*at her child,

a language yet to be for*gotten,*
or a body never dis*placed.* Sit—

w*here*? Where can we sit without
being moved, without being monstered?

What is a song worth singing here?
The silenced are listening.

What is a life worth living?
The caged want to know—and I, I confess

though free, desire to be freer.
Sit with me as I sit with that, the g*all.*

What is an hour well-houred? I abhor
both leisure and labour when I learn

everything carries a cost, every minute
must be accounted for, and extracted

from a pound of flesh. Despite this
my knees buckle for a fresh car*rot,*

the wet crunch of it & my muscles long
to ache, to grow, to slow, to age—

near a mountain or a river
somewhere flagless, uncountried

where I can say I am a hue, a being
a living breathing sea, immovable

& uncrossable, water calling to water,
a body still, host to a *kin*der universe—

you know, a sweet lie, something close
to true, but history keeps *proving*

I will do anything for a hunk of hard cheese
going green, even writing verses

for people who want to remember how good
they are, or were, or could be as *the*ir country

disposes others. Sit with me, please,
in the rising waters, as I sit with that.

No Context in a Duplex

'Tensions are escalating.' 'Mow the grass down.'
        Stretch past pain to find poetry, the way home.

            Pen the past to bind home. Write even the rain.
Israel, ghost nation, stains the orchards.

            Is rage enough to sustain a whole nation?
I dream of Palestine. Free, alive.

        Pull the line toward life, ask the dreamer:
Who gave the order, who profits from slaughter?

To make a border, make a slaughter.
            O history, O language, burst without love!

With love only, gauge the story—I said *with*
            Love—listen from the river to the sea.

            People riven from homeland list in grief.
Ten sons ululating. Mothers in the grass.

Draft

'Tensions are escalating.' Keep reading.
Tense ions embracing. Keep reaping.

'Tensions are escalating.' The words tremble.
Ten sons ululating. The world trembles.

'Tensions are escalating.' Don't ask why.
Ten suns excavating the sky.

'Tensions are escalating.' Nowhere to go.
Tenses enslaving. Refusing to future.

'Tensions are escalating.' They rise to fall
& rise in the fall & rise & rise & rise.

'Tensions are escalating.' All alone.
Teen sons. All alone.

'Tensions are escalating.' The rave begins.
Ten sins emulating. The grave begets.

'Tensions are escalating in Gaza.'
Ten sons are escaping in Gaza.

'Tensions are escalating.' I'm sick of this
grief, the endless revisions, my own

horrific eye.

My Enemies Need to Know

In the dark of our eyes we are together with the dead.

The last Arab was buried, and the war didn't end.

Not all the angels have averted their gaze in shame.

Hope is the measure of your spirit, and it is minuscule.

There is no distance that can outpace the call.

My ancestor is in your eyes. This is the reason I weep.

In prison, the condemned are known to repeat, I forgive you!

None of us have the keys to paradise, though the way is clear.

I can hear you calling for your mother.

The sounds of the world are receding. *I forgive you!*

I hear you calling me other. I forgive you If! Or

Give you I! fog your I! O figure O fury!

The sounds of the word are ceding. *I or you!*

Forgive I! Over you I vie! O grief O forge! I for you, give

The sun, the war, the seed. Whatever's left. It's all yours.

Don't worry about me. I am already in your eyes.

Shiver

There is a plague of mice
Eating through the hay.
A living wave of tiny teeth
Popping on the furry road.
Kill the little fuckers
Wipe them all out they say
Make bonfires of bone.
Out by Myall Creek I spy one
Crawling over a spent fire
Not to mourn its brethren
I think, just to be warm.

The Report

I am watching beautiful people
electrocute a man short-shackled
to the floor. Farmers call it hog-
tying. Language, I'm told, is built
to choose sides. What is meant:
the tool we believe connects us
maintains the divide. What I hear:
be careful of silence, what it holds,
how a word can take over your life.
I call my love tamale sometimes
because I want to eat her, and to place us
outside a language we know. She says
I smell like apricots in my sleep: I
harvest as I dream. This has little to do
with Adam Driver's *The Report*, nor
the fact it took years to discover torture
doesn't work—here we must ask what
work is, and whose hands are marred
by it—though there is an unconscious
field between the two, a supervision
homed between rapport and control,
a buried release. Everyone I know
loathes their work. Even the poets.
Everyone I know gasps for more.
I go to bed thinking of congress,
of the human in resources emailing
each killer their remittance advice
and at dawn my love reports:
what fruit I hold has gone to rot.

Workshop: Borders

For Alan Kurdi, and the unknown multitudes

I tell the students to write using only images. For example:

a mile of sand glistens
waves wash each grain blue
a small boy lies between the two.

When I say 'a small boy' we all picture
the same child
(the one who died) the one closest to us.

I fear the power of the image, how it changes nothing
except myself, how it is never just an image, how the boy lives
now under my bitten fingernails how

I live inside his grave, the great uncaring blue womb
of the world. I have been told to be more
specific: is the blue a) a sea b) a chlorinated pool c) an eye.

I tell the students language paves the way to every death.
Be careful with your rhetoric, especially when it feels right.
We cannot be picturing the same child.

We lack the imagination. We never saw him, not his life
or his headline. We looked away to practise
self-care. The timeline is too dark. Netflix and erasure:

a deluge of icons and canned laughter and bright graphics
and that ba-boum sound that lets us forget
there have been many more children dead in riverbanks

or swallowed by the ocean, unphotographed
in the desert, blown to pieces in warzones
or caged by we the civilised 'West', land of the damned

free. I tell the students to *move me,* and hope they cannot
hear the desperation. Teleportation
is all any of us truly desire: to move

and be moved, in complete stillness, collapsing distances
with a word, a shriven glance, an image
of a poet, in this case a man, bearded, Arab—I mean kind of

dusky, a faded beaten sky—surrounded
by students pale & dark & bored & solemn & on their phones
because this is important, and so not, and ugh

their rickety peeling tables forming a square
around the man, his vain efforts at peeling back the ocean
the seething black and green, the froth and heave of it

to cradle the boys and girls that never got to be so alive
as to be bored by a poem, the gravid magic of rhythm
given form, la ilaha illaAllah wu Muhammad r-rasul Allah

and doing his best, I swear, his best, to be professional
to not put his head on the damp shifting sand
and beg the waves to sunder.

Enough

Where was the poem when my uncle crashed to his knees
in his unfinished apartment, heart crumpling like cheap paper?

Where was it when my aunty heard the news
& began to keen in the kitchen?

When I see the sun fold itself into a messy napkin
I do not think of stanzas I assure you

there isn't a single thought in my head, not awe
nor singing, nor a sense of cosmic proportions.

There is only light, and its limits.

Poetry did not try to stop my mother from killing herself.
The ground did.

It caught her softly after she jumped.
When I began to dream of succeeding

where she failed, poetry did not save me.
I didn't get out a pen and a pad. I had no computer

to type on, nor a lover to sing to.
I had the night, and the memory of a laugh.

It was enough.
For a decade, it was enough.

In the Wake of a Tragedy

I asked God to sit with me
And He did. Suffering
Neither eased nor increased
For any of us, yet now
I still think twice before
I send another invitation.

Things that Saved My Life Lately

Dark rye toast with peanut butter. You know,
the thick tang of the nut on the mouth's roof.
The long lovely of close water: the deep green
canal, still, except where a shaggy German Shepherd
surges, only its head visible, as it struggles toward
the waiting leash. Further on, the bay, a blue feast
full of leaping fish and darting birds, white boats
and mirrored cloud. The water holding my worried
weight. You, queer boy. You, queer joy. Singing.
My father submerged in the curve of my smile.
The people searching for the possibility of a heartbeat
beneath the buried rubble in Beirut, day after day.
This list, for what it's worth, contracts and expands
like any heart, lately, small, wracked with tremors;
there remain the working men in high-vis vests, hot &
busy constructing detours for the walkers, the women,
the writers, around deadly ground. My mother, traumas
unresolved, and for whom, as much as love, I continue
to wade through the hungry hours, snout in the air, furious
in search of her hands, and what, together, we might unknot.

Love Poem for the Honeymoon Phase that Doesn't End

I look at you—and love.
I worry around this ease,
this intimate infinity.
Nor do I need my eyes at all

I think of you—and love.
This grace others my nights
the way freedom bothers
the long imprisoned.

There is too much space.
Life is endless in its potential
terrors. I hear you—and love
always, as an invisible

production, slow heaven
hard at work, asking:
When did I learn to value ache
over song? To struggle

to say a name without
spitting feels more honest
than the soft utterance of joy.
Or so it seems in a body

made by tragedy. Isn't it
possible love is easy
or else that I have worked
all my days and sleepless nights

for this and nothing else?
Isn't it possible we are worthy
no matter what, tell me the truth
no, wait, tell me what you trust.

On Finding the Prophet Muhammad (PBUH)
in Dante's *Inferno*

I romanticise the darkness of prison.
I say, everything becomes a marriage

in time, a marriage says what it must to survive.
My love, what are we guarding? Who has the keys?

I guard love, jealous as a key with one lock.
Value by exclusion is a jackal's game.

Losing is the name of the game. Value loss.
Abundance scares us. I fear what I feel.

I dance around fear, careful of us.
No boss, no timesheet, no clocking off

I'm on the clock, under the sheets, on guard.
This is what it means to be a settler.

What does it mean to settle in love?
I romanticise the darkness of prison.

Returning to Auburn, I Remember

I am happiest with a blade at my throat, a man in my ear. The barber was born in Iraq and around him are thousands of evil eyes, blue, to ward off evil eyes. Hundreds of prayer beads dangle down, from brown to black, jade to jewel. Waiting for a hand to wield them, to utter God's names and keep worry at bay. Hassan heaps my hairs, and from the back room the chirp of birds, the hymn of wings suffuses the shop. He would never keep a cat or a dog, he said. His birds need to be fed & watered & loved at least three to six times a day. Providing these ingredients keeps him occupied: a tap, seeds, conversation. The birds thrash at their cages, hooting & trilling & arguing about the definition of a sky. One says 'above', the others say 'a lie', say 'view', say 'inside'. Nearby, the mosque that briefly held my father in a metal casket, the masjid in which I mourn him, readies itself again for my regrets. I do not live here but I return to Hassan's hands, his trapped birds, to be shorn of my beard, to feel the boy inside, the night-gazing star-slumming cloud-shaper thrash in the back room for a drop, a seed, love.

Fruit

After my mother, who gave me the wounded earth
leaves my house, a stolen peach

in hand, and with only cherries to speak for her
presence, I shudder all over, again

at how close she came to knowing me.
I bow beneath the mercy of our separation.

It turns out language is good
for little except accumulating a barrage

of expensive fireworks & missiles.
Such ecstatic displays! Smell the cordite. Watch

the smoke become memory. Ya immi, won't you
take back these unforgiving waters?

As you return to your own lonely home,
past the tree you plundered of its fruit

won't you pause a moment to say, mother
to mother: I, too, have children

I tore into pieces.

Confession

It is easier to write about my mother
than to speak to her. I never want to
risk it. The horse's mouth isn't poetic.
It has taken chunks out of me.
I avoid going to where she lives.
I refuse to know the address
lest I walk there in my sleep.

Immi, I'm sorry I live
for poetry now. This is my excuse.
Your reality is no match for my memory
which comes to me with your face
sneering, where's the money, where is
the money in a sonnet you idiot.
You could have been more helpful.

For a Country that Cannot Keep Its Children

after Ghassan Hage

The day is forecast as catastrophic. Heat
strangles the sky. It bulges, a rotten purple.
Earlier, an old Greek and a friend unexpected
slipped into my sleeping throat to see
why I bulged, rotting within: a history
believed in, threatens to become faith
in a future—didn't anyone tell you
never to eat a seed? Oh it grows, it grows.
You must lose this weight to be at ease.
I rode the wind to another city
to tell it to get off my back, out my belly,
& it swallowed me whole into its riot
or Tuesday as it was better known, where
aunties & uncles circled to hold my nude
loving, my rude namelessness & we,
none of us truly family except in our living,
considered whether to kiss or kill
the soldiers in our minds. The country
burns still, and the smoke of it blurs blue ocean,
forest, fences. I mistakenly mow my neighbour's
yard. I weep into a stranger's handbag &
she says my son now is not the time for grieving,
it is the time for returning & this & this & this
is what bulges and burns: you refuse, again
to kiss your mother's feet.

Masks Off

Take me back to the slow murder of the globe
and the millions killed by American bombs and
diverse soldiers. Take me back to a simpler anger
with which I can sugar hell, and feed a trans soldier
before waving them off to kill children somewhere else.
No judgement! I, too, want to slit a sleeping country's throat
and this is how I know I am one of you. Fuck virtue
signals let's be villains. Oh habibi, take me back
to the dream in my father. Further, take my father
out of the grave and return him to Turkey, to home
before it was wreathed in flames. Take us back to dedde
working metal in Ceyhan. Take us back to his father
in Afghanistan, before he ran. Take us back to before
we had to run. God, please, take us back—or forward
to a day, one day, where my aunty isn't hungry in Lebanon
just a day, Lord, where this world is moved wholly by love.
And forgive me, until then, for not holding my breath
for still wanting even this colossal ruin.

VI

I Felt Like a Saint

The residency accommodated artists
for months at a time: a bedroom, a shower,
a kitchen, a studio, a haunting, snow.
Their internet smothered smut, tried
to keep me from being a slut. My love,
a world away, went hunting through
archives for the sex I described.
I felt like a saint, she told me, three
or more steps removed from desire,
crowned by a light that can only come
from sinning in another's place to know
their ache. For you, I will mouth a fantasy
halo, dribble, devour, suck. The law
of balance demands I devil your holy;
instead, I do nothing. Watch magpies
mating outside my window. Well,
the birds stood close, perhaps talking.
Unexpectedly, even magpies need
love. Never have I felt more perverse.
The space between us is full of bodies
paused. I jerk off just to feel normal again
and to honour her labour, the diligent
record of other people mourning
nude for the camera, all the little deaths.
Our screens stay dark, ecstatic portals.
You can be the patron of tribbing, I say.
I will be the song of absence.
Now press play on those men, please.

Chorus

Our bodies have been remade
in this new bed this door
we can open anywhere
on Earth we are opening
here, in this particular
way, and the way is soft,
the way is large and crafted
by many hands. Touch me
is the only chorus I know
that needs to be relearned
and the lesson can unlock
any life. My love sleeps
beside me her flesh held
by a desire greater than any
I can claim. O to be a longing
in someone else's body &
to cease when they are pleased.

Little Fictions

I am an inaccurate biographer
most days, indecisive and easily fooled
by three sisters: time, distance, light
each of whom love to lie
yet still I am named a prophet
of myself and the strangers
I lived beside or among for years.
I have become hesitant to speak.
I circle the truth until dizzy
with doubt and something new
comes of it, a fact not quite true
a resonant myth like Beirut
O she's a beauty, everyone says
particularly if you've never been.
I shouldn't care what you make
of my devastation—a fiction
because I live, as the moon lives,
diminished and full, once booted
or softly touched, called hoax
by the non-believers & holy
by witches, faggots, and foxes—
but I do. I blame Orhan Pamuk:
he made his innocent museum
real, a place you can trespass in
or enter with his work as ticket
and now, my god, I am afraid
of the permission I gave away,
the body in your hands, the faint
moan rising to my lips.

Rooted

It comforts to know trees can care
for each other. Beneath the earth
they hold hands, and even the stump
of felled oaks have roots that keep
them alive, a network that nurtures
the wounded. I wonder if a book
placed next to another can tell whether
it contains hurt, lines made of cut glass
and recollected knives, and if this is why,
after a length of time, all books lean
on each other. They may not grow or
have birds to house, still, they can speak
and record questions like, 'If a book
goes unread, was it ever real?' &
'If a book is read too much, is it super
natural?' To be read, to be real, red,
reeled, one word at a time into life,
is that not why I am here to begin
with, to be convinced a world exists
that I cannot see, just above my head
perhaps, airy, homely, green? I lie
in the clearing I call a living room.
I rest my back against my tall Billy.
I hold my own hands.

To Be Loved Like This

I loathe being outside when it rains.
Much like family, I can't see the beauty
when I am included. I love the subtle
work of water on windows, how glass
protects, separates, magnifies. It allows
us to hear the slop and splash on slopes
without rushing to be free of it, the slow
hard clasp of thirst. It reveals
the illusion of transparency. O shallow
curtain, I kiss it, mist it, get real
close to the muted crackle of droplets
meeting the world. Fields of popcorn.
What delicious entertainment, God is
saying, I am watching, I am falling
I am touching every inch of this earth.

Souvenir from Another Year

In the ancient temple by the sea seventy brown men
sing, then chant, the sound a risen many-limbed thing
that stalks into the stone amphitheatre to agitate
the audience, my own damp self among them, and I
follow the hum, I find the whole ritual performance
moving even though it's a top tourist attraction
and this context is meant to embed cynicism, the cash
that left my hands is meant to cheapen the experience,
to diminish the pink ribboning through the sky,
the unhurried wonder of water hazing cliffs,
the glint and shadow of a lone fishing boat tackling
distances, but the men and I, the summoned chorus,
care nothing for that. I finally understand that to be
moved is to not understand, at all, what has occurred:
it is to arrive in a new country as a strange animal,
unsure what happened to your mother, to your body,
to time—that vile woodpecker lapses into wounded
silence, a sweet abeyance—and even death takes
a smoke break when you are brought into a feeling.
I can't keep track of the story or the song, it leaps
from body to body, near-naked to costumed,
as I return, over and over, to the long sun
setting with blissful disregard for its freedom,
a serene fuck you to any poet or painter, daring
us to try to host such an ordinary image, a yellow
larger than our world, an everyday science fiction.
The men sing for an hour, for years & years, as women
glittering and golden, dance in perfect, terrible silence.

Another Faith

On the road home I pass the church
and the man with his god pamphlets.
I do not offer him my intimate eyes.
Opposite the man is the police station.
If he asked the officers, he would learn
I have my own prophet. I duck under
the laden willow—long silver lines
reach for my hair. Full of ancient music
I make it to my door and circle back.
On the second pass, I wave the man off.
On the third, I give him my first name.
On the fourth, he complains of his hip
and children who do not speak to him.
On the fifth, I ache, he aches, birds sing.
Each time, he tries to tempt me with God
and each time, I could kiss him. Such faith
in my holy lack, my deserving ungodliness,
such devotion to doubt could move the devil
to tears, but not I. On the sixth pass of this,
the world left to me, he asks why I continue
to walk, to torment him, my oldest friend,
with a soul he cannot save, and I tell him
I am out gathering the memories of angels,
which are always falling and always full,
I am soaked in this rain, look at my heavy
feathered head, look at what I weather,
and if you do, you will know why your papers
are meaningless. On the road home, the hard
final stretch, I am alone with the winged.

The Right Shoe

On the anniversary of your death I am reading my old poems to see if I
solved   grief
in them and forgot, or else let loose the solution to keep hold of the
enduring   ache
that took your place when you obliged the dirt & it turns out I have no
other   poems
only this one where I walk barefoot through the mall trying to find the
right   pair
of shoes, shoving one wide foot into each leather guess, an unbalanced
shade   denied
entry again, the textures a stricture, colours without closure, laced and
laceless   gods
without scripture. Forget about me, pity the clueless salesman with nothing
worth   selling—
he doesn't yet know there is no longer an earth to stand on.

Relevant to the Day
for Mr Daliri

After lunch, I decide I have no brothers and sisters, I am
Alone. My love is in another room.
She doesn't know of this yet, how far I have travelled

In the space of morning. Language no longer speaks to me.
Though I see its many bodies, I cannot be
Reached. When I return, I shudder in this God-given air,

Praise what remains. Outside, a man has built a kookaburra
Fifteen feet tall, and put a laugh inside
Big enough for the world. I watch as the icon meets its makers

And they join in laughing. You can inject this moment
With whatever amount of joy
Or poison you desire. I like to think the birds are not

Questioning if family is real, or joking about size—instead
They make a cacophony of kinship.
In the last human hour, I start to build a poem as large and

Weird as love. It cannot save us and still I am rushing
To usher every spirit to live within, to
Join in, to laugh, sweetly, at all that has transpired.

On Finding the Prophet Muhammad (PBUH) in Dante's *Inferno*

All books go blank, back to tree, back to snake.
     I am a snake and all the world a hiss.

          I whirl in this, part of what I make,
          kissing what issues forth. This means sound

has a body, a mother echo: I miss you.
     When two bodies meet, a recital takes place.

          My place was taken. I forget the words, sway.
     Quran means recite. Memorise the holy.

Memories are holy. Rescind to the mean.
     This is where I learn how to slither.

          On my belly, how I earn this story.
          The scales of justice dangle darkly.

          My scales sparkle among dark angels.
O tree, O Adam, beg me not to hiss.

On Finding the Prophet Muhammad (PBUH) in Dante's *Inferno*

I'm ashamed it took me so long
to anoint my body as capable of
saving anyone, even a number
of letters. Did I really go through
all the levels of one man's Hell
willingly, as if only a curiosity,
the luminous cavalcade of pain
unfelt, unacknowledged until I
came to a name I recognised
from my family's vocabulary
which some call history? A man
I am not allowed to recognise.
Forgive me, all I left behind—
now I know why I must return.

Believe

beliefs, sorry—lies my all put I
and language in

my those are these
:alone left dog

.for living worth is love
.for dying worth is Love

.us is world The
.dying always is world The

blame to all are We
.you forgive I

106

The Thing About Being in Love Is That

I pray every morning that I am buried first
& before I rise I lick the hardwood floors
that hold a memory of your feet.

I suck on the bulb of the sun outside
because it dares to know your hair
& to prove you out-delicious even the light.

I walk past the rotting hydrangeas in the yard
and brand the browning blue habibi
on the way to see Tolouli, who has owned

that word for as long as anyone I know—
do you see how love calls to love? Habibti
do you see how it gathers itself like rain?

It's not the dearest dialogue, habibi is
casual you know, a confetti endearment
& maybe this is why it is my favourite

the way it pours and hails out my mouth.
Inside my earliest memory of habibi
two sweetly huge men kiss hello

ya habibi my uncles or cousins or strangers
I'm not sure, but I was small and knew then
that anyone could be loved, if anyone

excluded my body. Now I sleep
and behind my eyelids, a habibi waits.
At home, the arguments, the dented

bed, the endless news, the horror,
the last pregnancy test—none of it
can alter the fact that ever since I met you

I darling the world.

Child

I lack the capacity for an unhappy
or disappointing experience this morning, I say

instead of, I need the slow death of routine
or, my body is the worst storyteller I know,

dog-earing the same books, glued to the re
wind. I wear my favourite masks, those that won't

provoke an attack, and preen within the trauma
called living. Stop pulling me toward the new

beloved. You hold the new inside you. It is ferocious
in its urgency. It will blaze through my old

which is the only land I know. Ash sweetens my lips
when we kiss. The new is coming, God help us, the new

revolves within us, the new will tear apart order
to be born, and then have the audacity to demand love.

Notes

My 'Upon Finding the Prophet Muhammad (PBUH) in Dante's Inferno' sequence is based on Canto XXVIII, in which Dante comes upon the Prophet in the eighth level of hell and describes his horrific torture. The language changes depending on the translator, though the scene remains the same. I reference Peter Thornton's translation, 'cleft from chin to colon'.

One of the poems in this sequence (page 70) references Noam Chomsky. 'Chomsky says persuasion is a soft violence'—I was paraphrasing what I'd read once, so I sent it to Chomsky to verify, and he replied, 'I wouldn't go so far as to use the word *violence*, but better than "persuasion", I think, is helping people to think things through on their own. A fine line.'

Four of these poems (three from the Upon Finding sequence) make use of the Duplex form, which was created by Jericho Brown, a melding of the sonnet, the ghazal, and the blues that comprises 14 lines of 9–11 syllables wherein the second line repeats and, in the repeating, changes.

The fourth example is 'No Context in a Duplex'. It was originally published online via Red Room Poetry, with the 'context' beneath the poem. As that was not the case here, I changed the title. The context is this: 'Mowing the grass' is the phrase Israeli forces have long used to describe their lethal bombardment of Palestinians. Writing this poem sickened me, even as I felt its necessity: to show the violence facilitated by language, the violence of metaphor. The Duplex as a form invites you to turn back to a line and, in turning back, change it—the line erodes in the echo, and becomes something new. Or not. Choosing when to allow that transformation takes on a devastating weight, a weight you are meant to refuse in making the last line a repeat of the first line. I chose to break that rule here.

Two poems are mirrored by an anagrammed version. This kind of anagrammatic poetics is also showcased in 'Relevant to the Day' / 'A Reimagining'. Lastly, this sequence—as well as the 'Relevant to the Day' poems—which employs the same title over different poems to oblique effect, was prompted in part by Terrance Hayes's superb book *American Sonnets for My Past and Future Assassin*. While not the first time I'd seen the technique, his use of it struck me the most forcefully.

'Redback' was written after Nikki Giovanni's famous poem 'Allowables'.

'Blessed Be This Sadness' was written after, and references a line from, Les Murray's poem 'An Absolutely Ordinary Rainbow'.

'Buzzing' and 'Believe' are lineated like The Arabic form, created by Marwa Helal, which subverts the Western gaze by forcing the reader to read the poem right to left. I choose not to include the Arabic footnote that is typically part of this form as, though I know the letters, I am not literate in Arabic. One day I might return to these poems and complete them.

'The Report' takes the line 'Farmers call it hog-tying' directly from the film. I used 'electrocute' to describe the shock of cold water being poured on a naked prisoner, Gul Rahman, in his unheated cell, who subsequently died from hypothermia.

'For a Country that Cannot Keep Its Children' is 'after' Ghassan Hage, the title came from a talk he gave in Granville. I wrote this poem afterward, with his permission to use the title.

'Relevant to the Day' (page 103) references Mr Daliri, an artist who built a fifteen-foot-tall kookaburra.

Acknowledgements

I'd like firstly to pay my respects to the Wangal and Wategoro clans of the Darug nation, on whose lands I live, and where I wrote many of these poems.

I could not have written this book without the Australia Council for the Arts, and my peers, who approved my grant. It allowed me to take my time producing this work and to give it a level of care that would not have been possible otherwise.

Thirty-two of these poems were originally published in some form by the following: *The Academy of American Poets* Poem-a-Day series, *Poetry London, Overland, Australian Book Review, Mizna: The Arab-American journal of art, Portside Review, Peril, Griffith Review, The Saturday Paper, The Spinoff, Cordite Poetry Review, Westerly, Djed Press, The Sunday Paper, Epiphany, Stillpoint, JustSmile, Wasafiri, Lickety Split, Australian Poetry Journal, Red Room's Poetry Month,* and *Arts & Cultural Exchange.* My thanks to the editors and producers of these organisations for their support.

I want to especially thank Toby Fitch, who edited this collection, for his excellent feedback, as well as my publisher UQP for their continued support. My thanks as well to Abdul Abdullah, the brilliant Muslim artist whose work 'a gentle nudge' graces the cover of this book.

My heart will always be with Naomi Shihab Nye, Kwame Dawes, Billy-Ray Belcourt, and Andrew McMillan for granting me their time, and their considered and kind responses to my work. It is an immeasurable gift to be in conversation with such extraordinary poets. My love to my poet-friends George Abraham, Marwa Helal, RA Villanueva, Mahogany L Browne, Ali Cobby Eckermann, and Caitlin Maling, for gracing my life with their light.

Twin spirits animated the heart of this book, and I owe them endless thanks: my father, for whom I still grieve, and my wife, whose love and kindness are incomparable. I live for her, and nobody else.

In this work, and all my work, I speak to many injustices in the world—from the individual, as with Gabriel Fernandez, to the systemic, as with the war crimes and crimes against humanity being perpetrated in Afghanistan and Palestine. One can never 'do justice' to subjects such as these, justice is an action to be applied in life, but at the very least I hope I have not done any additional harm to the communities my words touch on.

Literature, for me, is the province of elegy—and love. More than anything else, I hope my love has shown through.

Salaam,
Omar